heart breaks and cannon fodder

35 Years of Poetry by
Charles Lemar Brown

Broken
L
Press

To Whom It May Concern:

CONTENTS

INTRODUCTION

Oh, to be young again. Full of piss and passion, and the belief that every word, every idea that you held dear was worthy of nothing less than everyone's total devotion and attention. The belief that if you rebelled hard enough and long enough, your generation would accomplish what the generations before yours could not— changing the world. Or perhaps, like me, your desires were more simplistic. With pen and paper, one could take up the flame of those who went before— those great poets who inspired their generations.

George Bernard Shaw famously said that "youth is wasted on the young". And looking back, I can't say that I disagree with him. From a poetic standpoint, a youth's passion is so much hotter, their emotions more explosive, whether it be poems about sex, drugs, and rock'n'roll, or politically incorrect prose, youth holds nothing back. But with age and time, everything seems to become just a tad more mellow.

For the most part the poems within this book were written in the "wasted on the young" years of my life, to be more precise, the nineties. I was old enough to legally drink and young enough to think I had life all figured out. It was an amazing time. Ideas came and went at the speed of life, partially due I'm sure to my ADHD. A phrase here, a girl there, and news outlets everywhere, fueled the wanna-be poet who lived inside me.

Then at the height of it all, the bottom fell out of my wonderful world—divorce can do that you know. As I began to take stock of what I had lost, I realized that nearly all of my poetry was missing. And so, with heavy heart, I moved on.

Y2K did not get us and so I began to write poetry now and then, but never like I had in the nineties. Nearly twenty years and another divorce later, I found myself rummaging through a storage shed at my parent's home. In and amongst the pieces of furniture and boxes of forgotten keepsakes, I found an old metal suitcase. Inside was a little plastic box filled with three-and-a-half-inch floppy disks, one of which had the word 'Poems' written on its label.

Of course, I had to purchase a converter and wait for it to arrive, but when it did, there they were— my poems. As I read through them, it was like having a conversation with an old friend, or sometimes with lots of old friends. I had forgotten many of them. Some made me laugh. Some shocked the hell out of me. But all in all, they reminded me of the person I had once been and had lost somewhere along the way.

I was also reminded of a literature professor at Murray State Junior College in Tishomingo, Oklahoma who encouraged me to continue to write poems. And yet another professor, at the four-year university I attended a couple of years later that told me rather roughly that what I had was not poetry. It seemed he did not approve of my mixture of traditional forms with nontraditional themes or some such shit. I have since come to realize that if I may borrow a quote from Silvia Plath, "I am both worse and better than you thought." In other words, it all depends on who is reading the poem. And to be honest, on what day it is being read. There have been times when a poem has struck me as mediocre and two days later, I think, damn that's good.

What I have learned, however, is that writing, whether it be prose or poetry, novel or short story, if it is good, it will elicit either an emotion or a thought. It is my fondest hope that somewhere in the pages of this volume, you, the reader, will be able to find some bit or piece that stirs you, whether to laugh or to cry, or gasp in shock. And should you be inspired, because of some word or thought or idea along the way, to pick up a pen, or pencil, or laptop, and jot or type a poem of your own, I would be elated.

LUST, SEX, LOVE, & HEARTBREAKS:

True love, myth or not? The old romantic in me says it's possible, hell, there was even a time when you could have convinced me that I had found it, but alas, with age my philosophy on such matters has changed. I still think of myself as an old romantic, however, the realist in me, damn him, would insist that the heading above is more likely than true love—sex, if you're lucky, follows lust, and if your luck continues in time, you may even find love, perhaps even true love. And if you do, hang on to it with everything you have, for it has become a very rare thing indeed. More often, it has been my experience, both personal and witnessed, in the end a heart will break.

Now you may be wondering how someone so cynical could write love poems. Well, my friend, that is the beauty of it. All four stages listed above often elicit emotions, most of the time very strong emotions. And to a poet there is nothing more moving than emotion. Someone catches your eye and the poetic juices begin to flow. Like the birds and bees in springtime, lust is in the air. A good roll in the hay, or romp in the bedroom, does not always promote sleep, sometimes it brings out the poet. Then of course, there's the most fabulous of them all, the Love poems. The ones that come from deep within the heart. Those soul tickling emotions that make us all want to write sonnets like Shakespeare.

And for some, for the lucky few, love does indeed conquer all, but for the rest of us, we must address the fall—the heartbreaks. Yes, even in these, if we try, we can find poetry. I once saw an ad in the classifies of a paper in which a man was asking for a woman to date him and then break his heart. The ad did not say anything about the man's profession, but I was certain as soon as I read it that he was a Poet.

THE SUN OR A LADY

As I begin undressing,
  her warmth begins caressing,
My body from head to toe,
Lovingly touching my body,
  as she arouses my soul.
I experience pure ecstasy,
  in her warm caresses,
And heaven-sent rays of irradiance,
As lovely lines of silk,
  soothes my skin like mother's milk.

jolie ladie

Sunbaked leather features
Surround twin pools
Of crystal blue skies.
Weeping willow branches
Fall limp/red/dusty
Across the twin peaks
Of an old black Harley bra.
Beneath them a smooth desert plain
Extends southward
Towards a short stretch
Of faded blue denim
Tight and frayed at the edges.
The desert, hard and hot,
And still, I long to make the trip.

THE GOOD THINGS IN LIFE

Black lace stockings,
　High-heeled boots,
Tight red dresses,
　Tailor-made suits,
Rainy mornings,
　Starry nights,
Silky blonde hair,
　Sky-blue eyes,
A swayin' walk,
　A sexy smile,
A southern drawl,
　Lots of style,
Time on one's hands,
　Whiskey dry,
Smokin' cigarettes,
　An eagle's cry,
Lovin' any time,
　All ex-wives.
A few good things,
　In our lives.

A CRY IN THE NIGHT

She calls my name into the night.
                Is it worry? Is it fright?

She calls again and I go.
        Is something wrong?
                I tell her no.
                But she knows.

I lay down at her side,
And hope the darkness hides
My thoughts.

As tears fill my eyes,
I wonder,
"What will I do when her love dies?"

THE COLD DECEMBER WIND

A cold December breeze,
  Blew inward from the seas,
Gently spraying the old shoreline,
  As it softly whistled and whined,
Encompassing the soul and the mind,
Of the young man at the water's edge.
  Wrapped snugly in his coat.
He listened to its' silent voice,
  As it chilled his cheeks and chin and throat.
With inward strength and quiet dignity,
  He stepped swiftly in.
The water welcomed him,
And he escaped the cold December wind.

EUREKA

Refrain from quixotic foolishness
on Xanthippe-like women,
such endeavors are fruitless,
piss in the wind,
your baksheesh
of roses
or cards
or poems
no services will render,
but hashish and greenbacks
on Colfax in Denver
will bring out the nymphos
and a night to remember.

THE PRICE IS RIGHT

Her store,
a concrete square
around the streetlamp
at the corner
of 9th and Colfax,
her wares,
inside her arms,
between her legs,
for the right price
(a token really)
she'll sale you everything,
her heart,
her soul,
her body
for an hour,
No games,
No flowers,
No candy,
No trouble.

HELD FOR NAUGHT

Twenty years of laughter,
  Two decades of pain,
A mangled mass of metal,
  Love—a derailed train.

Refused to look at it,
  Crumbled steel and
      Tattered earth.
Tears and fears,
  And hearts that hurt.
Fix it. Fix it !!!
Wrap it up,
     it will heal.
One more Band Aid,
Time could fix it still.

No, okay, then …
  SCREAM !!!
Scream until you
     Have no voice,
Scream until your
     Mind is void.
Blow the tracks!!
Smash the train!!
Yeah …
  That'll stop the tears.
  That'll stop the pain. Wait. Just take a little,
  And Give a lot.
Remember what you
     Were taught.
Share the tracks,
Split the work.
Forget the pain,
Forget the hurt.

Oh, the hurt,
   The tears, the pain.
Rust, decay,
   Caused by rain,
The engine SINKS …
         Into the earth.
One more shot,
Another pill,
         But nothing works …

Now it time to move along,
   Let's clean it up.
It is what it is …
Shit happens. Life sucks.
Forget the train wreck,
That fight's been fought,
Twenty years over— gone,
All held for naught.

I SCREAM

I SCREAM!!!
    Then I SCREAM again!!!
LOUDER!!!
    LOUDER!!!
    Even LOUDER still!!!

The silence is deafening.
No one hears.
The rocks sigh…
The wind weeps …
The Earth stops …
And I SCREAM!!!

24-HOUR JUNKIE

As green as a bag of Mary-Jay
And just as intoxicating,
I sit around all day,
Just sit around waiting.
Like a junkie on a corner,
Hungry for a hit,
I'm hooked bad, addicted,
With no desire, no wish to quit,
To be close, to feel your presence,
This I need day and night,
Yes, I'm your 24-hour junkie,
And I need another hit,
    if that's all right?

alter idem

Eyes that stare into my soul,
Like mirrors on a wall,
Thrice I looked deep within,
Not believing what I saw,
And from that moment I cared not,
If the clock moved at all,
For the universe, so large and daunting,
Had become so very small.
A cozy little place,
No longer halved, but whole,
Completed by those eyes,
That looked deep within my soul.

beaux yeux

A star that burns a million years,
   Burns hot and dies,
Could never match the beauty,
   Of one look into your eyes.
A river cutting into the earth,
   A million years it tries,
But can never cut as deep,
   As one look into your eyes,
And should I live no minute longer,
   Before I meet that final demise,
I shall give thanks eternal,
   For each one look into your eyes.

WITHDRAWS

Your presence is requested,
  Nay, required,
No R.S.V.P. needed,
  Nor desired.
Don't bother to write,
And forget the phone calls,
You see, your presence is needed,
  I'm having withdrawals.
Sure, you voice on the phone,
  Makes the symptoms subside,
But they start up again,
  Soon after we say good-bye,
And the notes and letters,
  I'm afraid just won't do,
Because when I read them,
  I just want to hold you.
I'm afraid your presence,
  Is the only remedy,
For the symptoms of withdrawal,
  That are afflicting me.

THE SOURCE OF MY SEXUAL POWER

I can go on for hours,
Though I must confess,
It ain't 'cause I want to,
Or am unnaturally blessed.
It's just that the phone keeps ringin'
And there's kids at the door,
Left alone, just the wife and I,
I'd be done in three minutes, maybe four,
But constant interruptions,
Prolongs the deed for hours,
And leaves my wife a thinkin'
I have amazing sexual powers.

TO DRIVE A NAIL

The secret within the head doth lie,
Do not ask how, when, or why,
Just place your upmost trust,
In the masters' touch,
And have no fear of the size,
The master will fit it in,
Be it a six, an eight, or a ten.
Placement, now this is crucial,
And at times perhaps unusual,
But with proper care and thrust,
For the master knows these
    things can't be rushed,
In the end, all will be well,
But be forewarned, ladies,
Even a fool can drive a nail.

THE LYNX

Elusive as a lynx,
A mistress of desire,
Her dancing eyes beckon,
With passion and with fire.

Subtle hints surround her,
Like bees 'round a hive, they fly,
Oh, that honey so sweet,
Yet do I dare a try?

Failure at my door doth wait,
And a sting that knows no bounds,
Still, I long to loose that door,
And chance what comes around.

THE TEMPTRESS

As harmless as a rattlers' bite,
Your eyes entice my soul,
As bright as a moonless night,
You summons take their toll.
Beckoned by your constant stare,
I hear your call to go.
Oh, what would I find there?
Truly, I do not know,
But waiting, though such pleasant pain,
Has left a deep and empty hole,
And my mind, plagued by mental strain,
Though interested, still is crying no …

THE RIDE

Astride a great white horse,
For pleasure she doth ride,
With spurs upon her feet,
And six-guns at her side.
Her holster snug and tight,
Is also fur-lined,
And when she sets his saddle,
The horse may lose his mind.
For she rides quite well,
See how the lather doth rise,
Every time she climbs aboard,
And eases him between her thighs?

THE SONG

Your eyes are sparkling stars,
In a sky that's all mine,
Your smile is a fire,
That warms this heart of mine,
Your words are notes,
Sung soft and low and sweet,
Your voice the melody,
That makes the song complete,
And when I hear your song, I quiver,
For it touches me so deep,
That if a single tear is happiness,
I shall forever weep.

OKIE KNIGHTS

Chivalry ain't dead,
  It just changed its' dress,
So, ladies, here's what
  To look for when you're in distress ...
Wranglers that fit,
  Like a second skin,
Stetson hats,
  Mischievous grins,
Boots and chaps,
  Twinkling eyes,
Hearts as big
  As the Montana skies,
Laughter as smooth
  As wind through wheat,
Arms that can
  Sweep you clean off your feet,
Mr. Wrong,
  Dodging Mrs. Right,
That's what you look for
  In an Okie Knight.

GEMS

The treasure of the sea,
A drop of white from sand,
As precious as it may be,
Can never compare with
    One touch of your hand.

Diamonds on a beach,
As numerous as the sand,
As precious as they may be,
Can never compare with
    On touch of you hand.

A tower filled with gems,
From heaven to earth its' span,
And still I would not trade its' worth,
    For one touch of your hand.

THE DANCE

In the face of your beauty,
The sun can but pale,
For your beauty is such
That men would fight
   the flames of hell,
In hopes that a victory,
Would prove a chance,
To hold you in their arms,
If but for one dance,
And by grace and grace alone,
I alone have been blessed,
For in my trembling hands,
Your gentle heart now rests,
Nurtured by my care,
Guarded by my love,
And I give daily thanks
To the Lord above,
For bringing us together,
For giving me the chance,
To hold you in my arms,
As we dance this dance.

WHEN THE SONG IS OVER

Three verses to short,
And a chorus to repeat,
A tender touch and a kiss,
And the song is complete.

Beautiful as wind though trees,
The singers sing sweet melodies,
And each note, each word,
    Pulls at the heart,
Until at last it ends
    And the teardrops start.

The song is over,
But the music plays on,
Like your memories in my head,
That won't let me believe you're gone.

YOUR SWEET LOVE

If at this moment
  the world ceases to spin,
And the Earth and the heavens
  become as one again.
If the breath that I breath,
  I can do longer find,
Because the soul from within
  had left my body behind,
In blissful wonder,
  I will spend eternity above,
Complete in the knowledge
  that I have known your sweet love.

And if by chance
  one eternity ends,
And where it leaves off
  the next one begins,
Forever singing your name,
  I'll spend it above,
Complete in the knowledge
  that I have known your sweet love.

YOUR BEAUTY

Moonlight on satin,
An angel's smiling face,
And all the stars in heaven,
Can never replace,
The beauty I see
When I look into your face.

A fresh picked rose,
Spreads its' petals to the sky,
Eagles soar upward,
But no matter how they try,
Neither can reach the beauty
Of one look into your eyes.

So, from here to eternity,
Let every angel sing
Of the most wondrous
Sight my eyes have ever seen,
Of the love in your face,
And the beauty that it brings.

THE TOUGHEST RIDE

Tight stretched Wranglers
Two-steppin' by
Swayin' to the rhythm
Caught this ole cowboys' eye.

A shot a Jim Beam,
Courage in a glass,
Six guns ablazin'
I just had to ask.

Ten seconds later,
The shoot opened wide,
And this ole cowboys' heart
Began its' toughest ride.

GIVEN THE CHANCE

Moving a mountain
Would be an easy task,
All you need to do is ask.
Turning the tide,
No big deal,
For you, I could even
Make the Earth stand still.
These deeds, however great,
Could never define,
The feeling in my heart,
          In my mind.
To show that what I feel
For you is real, is true,
Simply put,
Given the chance,
I would die for you.

BEWARE THE RAINBOW

Love is a Rainbow,
Spread across the sky.
A distraction,
An illusion,
That fades away with time.
A brilliant band of color,
That leaves you searching
    For the end.
Yes, love is a Rainbow,
So, Beware the Rainbow,
    My Friend.

I WISH I COULD TOUCH A STAR

If I could touch a star,
I'd change the way we are,
Alter the places that we've been,
And put the pieces together again.
Oh, what a Paradise it would be,
And I would take you there with me.
Yes, but wishing,
        that's the easy part.
And Reality,
Now there's where
        the heartaches start.
So, please forgive me,
        for the way we are,
And know,
I really do wish I could touch a star.

liberum et solum

Where do you go
    When you can't go home?
Everywhere and nowhere,
    You just roam and roam.
One step ahead of trouble,
    Two steps behind,
One step from insanity,
    Slowly losing your mind.
Out on the road,
    Free and alone,
That's where you go,
    When you can't go home.

The Flower and the Rose

With humility and strength,
  He raised his withered head,
Winked up at the bright red rose,
  Smiled and softly said,
"Yesterday, when I was young,
  Oh, how I wish, I had known
              You then,
For, I would have charmed you,
  And tried your heart to win.
But, alas, Sweet Rose,
  I must regrettably decline,
For today, is your day,
  As yesterday was mine.
So, as your petals blossom,
  And mine begin to fall away,
I mourn my loss of yesterday,
  And bid you, pleasant day."

DREAMIN'

If you were a dream,
I'd dream only you,
And sleep day and night,
My whole life through,
And if I were a rose,
I'd bloom just for you,
And imagine your kisses
In the moist morning dew,
And if I were the sun,
I'd rise at dawns' song,
And watch only you
The whole day long,
And envy the moon
When the day was through,
For the hours of darkness
When he watches over you,
And if you were a dream
I'd dream only you,
And sleep day and night,
Forever with you.

FOR AN ANGEL

Angels live in Heaven,
  Souring upon high,
  Playing golden harps
  On pure white wings
  They fly,
But Heaven ain't
  The only place
  Angels can be found,
For now and then,
  They walk on Earth,
  Both feet upon the
  Ground.
No halos.
No golden harps.
Yes, it's the honest
    Truth,
Not all angels have wings
  And you are living proof.

WHEN I LOOK AT YOU

A sweet red rose blooming anew
  Kissed by the morning dew,
As lovely as it may be
  Can never match the beauty
I see, when I look at you.

Dawn rising upon the ocean blue,
  Painting streaks so sweet to view,
As wondrous as it may be
  It can never match the beauty
I see, when I look at you.

So be my days many or few,
  This I know is true,
Happiness for me will be
  Each day to gaze upon the beauty
I see, when I look at you.

I HELD AN ANGEL

I held an angel in my arms,
For just a little while,
Kissed her lips,
Caressed her cheeks,
Watched her as she smiled.
Yes, I held an angel in my arms,
And then today, she flew away
Leaving me here alone
With memories of a happiness
That I had never known,
And though I know
She had to go,
I know it had to be,
I shall love her ever
Through all eternity.

The Path to Bliss

Like lightning
And a lightning bug
We're like
A kiss and a hug.
A little caress,
A little duress.
A little flash
Some rolling thunder
A mighty crash
From liking to loving
To chewing ass mad
And then right back
To what we once had
A rollercoaster ride
From start to now
And love survived
Through it all somehow
And two lightning bugs
With a hug and a kiss
Forget the madness
Enjoy the bliss.

I Just Know

Deep within my Heart of Hearts,
   Deep within my Soul,
In the place where I hold
  Things most dear,
      I Know…

Beyond all Explanation,
   Beyond reason or control,
In the place where I hold
  Things most dear,
      I Know…

I say "I Love You."
   You wonder How I know.
In the place where I hold
  Things most dear,
      I Just Know.

I Love ...

the way you stretch and smile
   when you sleep until ten.
the way you hide and groan
   when you wake up before then.

long walks on the beach
   with your hand in mine.
the hypnotic sway of
         your sexy behind.

your body, your laugh,
   your kiss, your touch.
You, everything about YOU,
   and everything about US.

Love You Forever

See that mountain,
    I can't move it,
And the tides
    I can't control,
But I will
    Love you forever,
    This much I know.

I can't make
    You love me back,
And your trust
    I may never know.
But I will
    Love you forever,
    Out of control.

I don't have a clue,
    Don't have a plan.
I make mistakes,
    I'm not Superman.
I can't give you awesome,
    Can't fly high above,
But I'll adore you forever,
    And give you ALL my love.

You Are The Sun

Love is an endless bag of seeds,
    That we plant as we go.
Faith is the rain that falls,
    To help the flowers grow.
Hope, well hope, is the light
    That caresses from above,
    Gives the flowers life,
And fills the world with love.
And so, as I plant the seeds,
            one by one,
I pray when the rain falls,
    You will see what I've done,
For in this world,
    In my world,
            You are the sun.

From Afar

I dream of moments
We never share
And adore you from afar
But fall silent
When you draw near
For I remember who you are
The brilliance
At break of Day
My sun
My moon
My star
And I, night's Shadow
Hopelessly fading away
A smile
A nod
A heartbeat
And once again,
I adore you from afar.

Love

Love heals some;
For others,
It is only pain.
A cracked heart
That bleeds
Yesterday's wine,
Fogs reality,
And muddles
The mind.

Love frees some;
For others,
It is a prison.
A wired cage,
A home of such
From which to view
A world
Safe from
Its touch.

And I,
I am caution,
Who stares
Through the bars,
Drinking my wine,
And avoiding
Its scars.

My Heart

Please do not touch me there
Anywhere but there
This heart is in need of so much repair
It is broken bleeding
Shattered needing
Love and tenderness
Spiritual superglue
More or less
Torn and tattered
A total mess

It is bruised
Black and blue
Faded to yellow
Hard glass
Soft jello
A spoonful of hurt
Rub some dirt
On it
Forever
Eternity
Just quit

It's not real
Needs time to heal
Kiss me …
Caress me …
Feel
Free to undress me,
But, please, don't touch me
There …

tempus sese

Shiny armor
  And a noble steed,
Don Quixote
  Ain't got shit on me.

A life of
  Savin' damsels
      In distress,
Has left me
  Brokenhearted,
One fucked up mess.

Too old,
  To do it anymore,
Your help,
  I must implore.
So, if you see me
  In knight's attire,
A hero riding forth,
I ask a single favor.
Please, I beg of thee,
Shoot the fucking horse.

Eternity

Eternity would seem,
  Oh, so brief,
Wrapped in the love
  Of your arms.
For time doth
  All but cease,
When I'm trapped
  Within your charms.
So, let the world
  Around us spin,
And the days and
  Years slip by,
For I care not
  If it ever ends,
As long as there is
  You and I.

Halos and Barbed Wire

Golden halos and rusty old barbed wire,
Sometimes the two entwine.
I know for an angel
Fell into these arms of mine.
Just a simple ole Okie
In ragged boots and jeans,
Staring into heavenly eyes,
Holding every cowboy's dream,
And I thank the Lord above,
For sending me such sweet love,
And forever bless the time
When a golden halo
And this rusty ole barbed wire
Became eternally entwined.

CONFESSIONS

Most times,
    I sleep the whole
        night through,
But now and then,
    I dream of you,
And most days,
    I just do what I do,
But now and then,
    out of the blue,
I'll see something
    and think of you.
They say,
    time heals all,
And maybe,
    That's true,
But every now and then,
    I still miss you.

Loneliness

If loneliness had wings
It would fly away.
If anger could sing
It would scream all day.
Metallica in the morning,
AC/DC at noon,
A little Kiss at dusk,
Then Twisted Sister
  Under the moon.

If loneliness had wings
It would fly all day.
A huge dark thing
Screaming like a jay.
An old blue jay,
High in a tree,
Screaming
THIEF!
  THIEF!!
    THIEF!!!!
You stole
Happiness
From Me!

But loneliness has no wings,
So, here it will stay,
Terribly silent
All the long day,
And I will wrap it around me
Like an old worn cloth,
And try to forget
All the things that I've lost.

Beautiful Zombie

As cold as a corpse
With the heartbeat to match
And yet somehow
You still manage to attract
The eye of everyone
You pass by
It's easy to see
The how and the why
For your beauty
Is truly something to behold
As it conceals the
Fact that you have no soul
Some will say I'm bitter
But it's not that at all
It's just that I've been there
To see the curtain fall
And watched in horror
        And delight
At the darkness and
        The light
As it twirled and twisted
In an eerie dance
And like a fool
Thinking I had a chance
I offered my heart my soul
        my all

Me, bitter, no, not at all.
For I am at fault
I'm the one to blame
I was the one who
Chose to play your game
Lose, win, die or draw,
Live love, fly or fall,
Crazy?
Maybe
Insane?
Yeah,
For sure.
Wait …
Please hand
Me my crayons
Before you
Shut the door.

Setareh

A single diamond
In a sea of black ,
Or simply fate
And no way back?

Deepest night,
Or brightest Day?
Kismet or Karma,
Which would you say?

A smile or a kiss
Or a simple
   Handshake?
Love that will
   Last
Or just
   Another
     Heartbreak?

Dare I trust?
Dare I try?
Or should
I just let you
Walk on by?

Are you my
  Fate?
Or a simple
  Night ray?
For your
  Answer I await.
Speak to me,
  My beautiful
      Setareh.

Real and unreal

I cannot believe how real it was
then how unreal it got
real was a little slice of Heaven
unreal, well, it definitely was not
Real was the way you looked at
   me the first time that we met
Unreal was how quickly you
   looked away as soon as
   our lives were set
Real, eternity won't be
   long enough
Unreal, forever is over,
   goodbye my love
Real the tears that
   fell like rain
Unreal, the emptiness
   and the pain
Real the finger pointing
   and the blame
Unreal, I will never
   be the same
Real, life is both
   Real and Unreal
Unreal, the way I
   no longer feel
or even care
   if it's the real
or the unreal
that is fair

Unreal, time heals all
Real, the new tears
   that begin to fall
And water the
Unreal scars
On this real heart
That is breaking
Apart
Unable to
Separate the
Real from that which
Is not
No,
I cannot believe how real it was
And how unreal it got.

Half Empty or Half Fool?

Half empty or half fool?
Let's put it to the test.
Half Empty is this heart
   that once beat inside my chest.
Half fool is how I feel
      on days that I'm at my best.
Half Empty is the pillow
         on her side of the bed.
Half Empty are the shelves
      in the left side of my head.
Half empty is the hour
Half fool is the minute
And all the power
And all the hurt Within it
That empties the heart
Completely
Of the half-wit fool
That meets me daily
In the mirror.

Half empty or
Half fool?
Does the answer
Draw nearer?
Both you say,
And I concur,
For I am both
Half empty
And half fool
Without her.

POLITICALLY INCORRECT & OTHER CANNON FODDER

Cannon fodder is a term used for soldiers who are considered expendable material during a war. During the American Revolution, soldiers from each side lined up and took turns firing at each other. They were cannon fodder, the first to die from musket fire and cannon blasts. Today this style of fighting seems silly to most of us. Why would anyone agree to stand on the front line in plain sight and allow someone to shoot at them? And yet, in a political sense, the largest percentage of the world's population can still be classified as cannon fodder. We are the expendable masses. Folks who work forty, sixty, eighty hour a week jobs, so that someone on the other end of the income spectrum can sit high on a hill and maintain control.

In my early twenties I had a revelation—those in control, those high up on the proverbial hill, use social media like smoke and trick mirrors to keep our attention on whatever fabricated crisis will keep us from asking questions they have no desire to answer. One of their biggest thrills is to pit common people against each other. Over the years, I have seen race, color, gender, sexual orientation, and political affiliation used to distract the masses.

We sure like to pick sides. And we can only like those who are on our side, right? Hey, I don't make the rules—in fact there are those who would say, I don't even follow them very well. I would like to tell you that I have all the answers. That I know how to accomplish world peace. I do not. And with that said, I must tell you that most of the poems included in this section were written during a period in my life when I was certain that by the time I reached my current age, I would have done all the work necessary to mend all of the divisions in this world. Oh, the ignorance of youth.

A BATTLE CRY

Moments are awastin'
  Time for rest is past.
Man your battle stations,
  It's time to kick some ASS!

The enemy is among us,
  He knows our every flaw.
It's time we stood up to him,
  Let's kick him in the balls!

Prejudice knows no mercy,
  So, we shall show him none.
We'll drive him, drive him, drive him,
  Until the job is done.

So, man your battle stations,
  Time for rest is past.
Moments are awastin',
  It's time to kick some ASS!

THE PROSTITUTE

Society is a prostitute,
Playing on a golden flute,
Luring men with sexy charms,
Into her widespread arms.
A wolf, dressed like a sheep,
Intelligently, she keeps the price cheap,
So, men will think her a playful tramp.
Beware you fools, she is a vamp,
That sucks your life blood dry,
And leaves you empty…until you die.

THE SPARROW

As I walked along one day,
A sparrow stole my thoughts away,
And forward to the future flew,
A decade passed and then two.

In an unknown city he finally perched,
And through his eyes I slowly searched,
For signs of hope for those to come,
Then silently wept—for there were None.

A solid white line ran through the city's center,
And all along the line signs reading—DO NOT ENTER.
All those whom I saw to the line's right,
Were of one color and that color was white,
And to the line's left the problem grew worse,
For the sight was the same—only reversed.
Blacks to one side—Whites to the other,
Each in his own world, no need for the other.

"Has prejudice succeeded?!!!, I felt myself cry,
"Is our country dead? Or just about to die?!!
Panicked, I snatched my thoughts back through time,
And tucked them safely in the back of my mind.

Each time I see a sparrow now,
The vision slips out, somehow,
Escaping from its' hiding place,
And brings a tear—that descends, slowly—
                    Down across my face.

ONE PEOPLE

Red, yellow, black, or white,
  Which one is right?
Perhaps, all are wrong,
  One people, singing different songs.

THE CAGE

Deep within his heart,
　　There is a yearning to be free.
The metal cage restrains him,
　　As society does you and me.
Escape for him is useless,
　　They'll only bring him back.
Nothing is ever free,
　　From society's enormous sack.
Conform! Conform! Conform!
　　Or else you are no good,
And if you should refuse,
　　You'll wear the cracker's hood.
Theirs is the only way,
　　It has to be the best.
You will see it that way,
　　To hell with all the rest.
So, there he sets,
　　Behind his metal bars,
And we go their way,
　　And avoid the battle scars.

THE BEAST

From the edge of the wooded darkness, he looks in,
At the beast filled with evil, filled with sin.
The wireless cage secures it with a constant grasp,
Forever, through the ages and from the past.
His nostrils flare, repulsed by its' eminent stench,
Filth covers its' giant body, every square inch.
Inside its' massive gut maggots crawl around,
Feeding on its' flesh, from toe to crown.
From the darkness he steps into its' stinking pit,
Crossing the thin line between him and it.
Its' gigantic jaws close over him like a huge net,
And once again he becomes its' pet.

ZEBRA STRIPES

Zebra stripes are segregated,
And greatly appreciated,
By ignorant men.

TO YOU, FROM US

You had your chance, now give us ours.
We will not rot behind your bars,
Imprisoned by your dead Ambitions.
Go fuck yourselves! Go fuck traditions!

HELP US STAND

Mothers, fathers -
Guardian of all kind,
  Do not tamper with our minds.

Help us,
  Blow the ember,
    Feed the flame.
Share our errors,
    Share our fame.

We will find our own dreams,
              Our own ambitions.
Do not force on us those old traditions.

Together we shall soar higher,
              Hand in hand.
Do not push us forward,
              Just help us stand.

WE, THE PROSTITUTES,

She sells her wares beneath an old streetlamp.
She is a professional, a professional tramp.
Her wares are home spun, her very own charms.
Her Office is between her legs and inside her arms.
We scoff at her business, laugh at her plight,
Judging her wrong, judging ourselves right,
But she is no different than you or me,
She too is a slave, slaving for Mr. Pimp Society.
She pedals her wares, and we pedal ours,
Each dreaming of a day filled with stars,
But it never comes, we get the old axe.
Mr. Pimp smiles and calls it a tax.
She sales her body, we sale our lives
To get ahead in the struggle and strife,
In truth and all actuality,
We are all Mr. Pimp's prostitutes in reality.

THE BONSAI REBELLION

At birth they put us in little clay pots,
And feed us heritage and traditional rot.
Trimming our roots and trimming our limbs,
They keep us within our little pots' rims.
We learn their truth; we learn their lie.
We are society's little bonsai.

Break the pot!! Break it from rim to rim!!
Stretch forth your roots! Stretch forth your limbs!
Upward and downward, stretch yourselves about!
Do not fear to scream the rebel's shout.
The time has come for the new generation,
Go find Yourselves without hesitation.

When the keeper of the pots asks, "Why?",
This shall be our battle cry,
"We are the new generation, come to kick down your door!
We will be your bonsai no more!!!"

RULED BY 7000

As he sets upon the white house roof and masturbates,
On his head, sweat begins to precipitate.
The crowd below screams and yells,
As he shots forth a million cum cells.
His 7000 leaders' elite,
Stare down at the masses in the street,
Cheerfully wallowing in the semen shot forth,
From their figure head far above the white house porch.
America the great, Land of the free,
Ruled by 7000 through the fucking TV.

RECONSTRUCTION TIME

Dirt, Filth, Destruction.
Time for reconstruction.

They sit on their candy asses,
Ruling the public masses.
The great, the mighty, the elite.
Hey, look at us down here in the street,
Scrimping and scrapping
   For nickels and dimes.
   Reconstruction time.

Its' engine is old, its' oil leaks.
25 MPH max, that's its' peak.
It runs around town never getting out.
How will it ever hear the public's shouts
   For nickels and dimes?
   Reconstruction time.

Redo it, make it new.
Overhaul it through and though.
Make it great in all the states,
Do whatever it takes,
To decrease the public's shouts
   For nickels and dimes.
   Reconstruction time.

SCREAM
for Rodney King

My skin may be white from where you stand,
But my soul is red, white, black, yellow, and tan,
And it issues an angry barbaric scream,
At the reality of society's terrible dream,
Of a country ruled solely by the white.
The silence is over, I'm ready to fight,
To right the wrongs of generations of hate.
I will start today and hope it's not too late,
To undo the terrible things that have been done,
Terrible horrible things that cover my sun.

I am America and I am mad.
The white man's reign is pitiful and sad.
They've trodden on my people, they, the majority.
They've penned up the race that had seniority.
They've freed the black man, but keep him in chains,
Caring not about his sorrows, not about his pains.
You are a wicked people; you've made a wicked race.
Get out you so-called elites, you're going to be replaced,
By a people with a soul, a people with a heart.
We've come together now to make a new start,
To build a country where no man will be beaten down,
By badged men's batons and the elite's great crown.
A country where justice is preserved,
And no rights are reserved,

For the slime, and the trash, and elite,
That beat a man down in the street.

I am America, I am brand new,
Ruled by many, not by a few.
I am America with all new places,
Land of many people with different colored faces,
Land of many, but a single race,
Prejudice is extinct, it has no place,
In my great country, in my great states.
I am America, the United States,
Home of the free, land of the brave.
I am America freed, no longer your slave.

YOU'LL NEVER KNOW

He smoked some pot,
   but didn't inhale,
And even if he did,
   What the hell,
Maybe it's time
   we had a few leaders,
Who didn't hang
   like old dead peters,
On racist traditions,
   and the elite's ambitions,
But stayed stoned
   off their asses,
And listened
   to the masses
Down in the streets.
   Fuck the Elites!

We are the many,
   they are the few.
It's time to elect
   somebody knew.
Somebody who will
   stand behind the races,
Not matter what
   color their face is.
Hand me a joint,
   I'll run this show,
And if I inhale,
   hell, you'll never know.

THE CRACK

The crack is wide and deep,
And grows wider as we sleep.
Awaken America!!!

THE GREAT BLACK DOVE

America the great, land of the free,
    Where the masses bow to the great elites,
    Who know nothing of our plight in the streets,
But simply rule our great society
Through the mind-draining screen of our TV.
    Listen, listen you so-called elites.
    We are the people down here in the streets,
Those who touch and smell and hear and see,
The evil your pitiful reign has done,
    While you sat content on your throne above,
    Content that nothing under your great sun,
    Would ever challenge you so far above.
Beware, there is something new under your sun.
    The New Generation, the Great Black Dove.

WHITMAN, FROST, GINSBERG, AND ME

Old Uncle Walt, with his visions of an oversoul,
Thought we all had a purpose, a goal.
He thought America was wonderful, America was great.
What would he think now of our great states?
Where black men get beaten down in the streets,
And the whole damned country is ruled by 7000 elites.

Mr. Frost, he hated fences most of all.
Well, Mister, they tore down the Berlin wall,
But another grows wide and tall,
And affects us, one and all.
An invisible barrier between the races,
Grows higher than the heaven's face is.

And while Ginsberg saw his generation wasted,
I see mine being basted,
Like microwave dinners,
No losers, no winners,
Just masses, masses down in the streets,
Being slowly basted by the great elites.

Put away your butter and your bureaucratic pen,
We may be expendable masses, but we are still men,
And we the bungled and the botched from your cities' streets,
Will band together to smash you, you so-called elites.

YOU WITHOUT SIN

You have condemned her, you without sin,
Because she aborted the fetus within.
Never did you stop to think, to care, to ask,
About her pain, her sorrow, her past.
You simply called her evil
   And condemned her to hell.
Well, who in the hell are you
   That you can so easily tell,
That this young woman,
   Heartbroken, in pain,
Is really the one who is to blame.
You know nothing of the man
   Who forced her legs apart,
Penetrated her body, ruined her soul,
   And destroyed her precious heart.

You know nothing of the demonic father she had,
Who beat her, abused her, and said she was bad,
Or the five bastard children,
    At her house right now
That she must feed and clothe,
    Though she doesn't know how.
So go, go screw yourselves, you without sin,
Had you been her, you would have aborted
    the fetus within,
But you are you and she is herself
    and who can tell,
If she has already paid for her sins
                And
If it is you who will burn in hell.

THREE CRAZY BIRDS

Three crazy birds sitting high up in our old oak tree,
Squawking, scream down at me.
They shout of war and rape.
They shout of murder and hate.
With tones so hateful and belligerent,
They scream until my patients are spent.
Arguing between themselves and with me,
They rant and rave and shake the old tree.
Losing my grip, I slip free.
Falling, floating to the ground,
And laying here I have found,
Others, who like me,
  Have been brutally shaken
    From our beautiful old tree.

I WILL FIGHT YOU

You rear your ugly face,
And laugh at my brothers' plight.
I curse your ugly face,
And join my brothers' fight.
Hitler is dead.
He is dead and gone,
And you,
   you help his dream grow strong,
And, although,
   I am but one,
I will not rest,
   until I can no longer fill the sun
Warm against my skin.
I will fight you, fight you to the end.

TO WHOM IT MAY CONCERN

You've made peace with Russia
and
won the Gulf War
and you're oh so proud of yourselves,
we're sure,
but what have you done for US lately?

You ignored us,
like some teen-age kid,
so we over spent our allowance,
yes we did.
At first you refused to believe it,
said something was wrong with our budget,
and then a short time later,
you saw it was true,
so you tried to make the allowance brand new.
If you had only been here from the start,
You wouldn't have this pain in your heart.

Yes, you ignored us,
so we fought with our brothers,
calling them names and cursing their mothers,
then when violence broke out
and
a town went up in flames,
you pointed at us,
said we were to blame,
now ain't that a shame.
If you had only been here from the start,
you wouldn't have this pain in your heart.

So what are you going to do for US now?

SPOTLIGHT THE SIN

Smoggy, gray clouds
Of mankind's prejudice
Roll through the skies of our minds,
Hiding the scene
Of the morning sun,
Dawning on a new day
That has begun to shine
On the elite's asinine plan
Like a spotlight
On the playwright's lead man.

A plan filled with sorrow and degradation,
That will segregate this great nation,
Labeling women and men,
By the color of their skin.

This is not a plan, this is a sin,
And so, we pray for the rain and the wind,
Let it blow and let it descend
On the clouds of smog and clear the nations skies,
And spotlight the master elite's lies.

Then, and only thin will there be
Harmony in our streets.

I AM THAT STONE

A stone drops into the water
and the ripple begins

to expand outward

from the spot

of contact.

The ripple grows wider

as it goes, causing the circle to grow.

I am that stone!!

YOU HOWL, I SCREAM

Three decades have come and gone
Since Ginsbergs' generation was wasted
And still we go on living a Coca-Cola existence.

O'Captains, My Captains! I sing your songs
And hear them echoing in the trees.
I too am tired of being screwed
By the seven thousand pagan pigs that rule our lives.

I long to set with wiry Old Uncle Walt,
        And talk of his universal soul.
I want to smoke Ginsbergs' plant,
        Get high and discuss Perot.

My generation too has gone to the dogs,
And the catcher now looks for me,
My spirit is all I have for a cloak
And should I lose it, I will become like the
        rest of my fellow humans,
An Invisible Man, no longer running from the beast,
But a part of the despicable, disastrous machine.

A second, a minute, an hour, a week, a month, a year, a decade,
a century, same shit, different millennium.

You howl, I scream. You die, I dream.

Wasted, basted, we live for weekends.
Seven-day coach potatoes.

America the beautiful, Land of the FREE.
Just Do It, Rat Race, Monopoly.

Monogamy is right, fornication a sin.
Monogamy is as common as virginity is.

The Heartbeart of America! A fucking car!
You've Come A Long Way, Baby! NOT!!!

You howl, I scream. You die, I dream.

THE ELEPHANT PRAYER

Welcome to the Circus,
The clowns come marching in,
Step right up! Sit right down!
It's all about to end.
Your comfy little tent,
So bright, so neat, so clean.
Your sweet little life,
So quiet and so serene.

Just set and watch the clowns,
They're here to make you laugh,
To forget about the Elephants,
Future, Present, Past.
Now the clowns,
    They are a 'fleeing,
"Oh Dear, Oh Dear,
    The Elephants are here"
And everybody laughs…

Now the Elephants are screaming,
    And we are as well,
The tent is falling down,
    And all has gone to Hell …

The Elephants are gone now,
And the clowns,
  They can't be found,
The circus is quiet,
We're coming back around.

It's time to get on home,
In time the wounds will heal.
Time to move along,
But it all seems so unreal.

Yes, the Elephants are gone now,
Let them not return again.
Please, Lord, I pray thee,
  No more Elephants,
We have seen enough of them.

Our World

Break out the canvas,
    Raise it High.
Cover up that
    Pale gray sky.
Have another drink.
    Dull the pain.
Brace yourself,
    Here comes the rain.
Feel the old girl
    Pitch and sway.
Welcome to Our World,
    It's a Circus Everyday.

Enter the Elephants,
    A distraction you see,
Then,
    Lions and tigers, and bears,
    Oh My, Oh Me.
Now That's Entertainment ! ! !
    Or so you say.

Welcome to Our World,
   It's a Circus Everyday. Let's give'm a show.
   Bring the house down.
You be a Super Hero,
   I'll be a Clown.
We'll swing on the trapeze,
   Walk the High Wire,
Jump though flaming hoops,
   While juggling fire.
Entertain 'em, Educate 'em,
   And send them on their way.
Yep, Welcome to OUR WORLD.
   It's a Circus EVERYDAY.

Squirrels

Both a blessing and
  a curse.
Life at its best and
  at its worst.
So, cool my
  Superpowers,
Like entertaining
  myself for hours,
Watching squirrels
  that only I can see.
Oh, but don't
  envy me.
It's those same
  little creatures
That had all my
  teachers
Running for the hills,
And asking my mom
About meds and pills,
Throwing around words
Like acceptable and normal,
Treating me like I'm diseased,
When I'm actually Supernormal.
After all how many
  squirrels do they see in a day?
And who are they to judge?

Who are they to say,
That because I do not
  fit society's norm
That I should be the one
  To conform?
Fuck them!
I am me,
  and that's exactly
  who I am supposed to be.
Maybe erratic and hard to control
At times withdrawn
  at others too loud and too bold
Yeah, sometimes it's a curse,
  and sometimes a blessing,
But I am who I am
  thanks to my ADHD.
So, love me or hate me,
It will be what it will be,
And whichever you choose,
You'll still be you,
And I'll still be me,
And the squirrels you miss,
I will surely see,
And thanks to you,
There will always be,
      more squirrels for me.

(stupid suckers)

I wish I had a car
and nowhere to go
I'd drive to Kansas
and fuck Toto
and Dorothy
and Auntie Em
and Wilma Flintstone,
Betty Rubble and Pebbles
all at the same time
and then 1,994 more
willing women
by then with any luck
I will have contracted
the HIV virus
and can write a book
telling how sorry I am
and when ten million people
buy it I can set back with
my million dollars and laugh
(stupid suckers)Or maybe

I'll drive to Ark-Cans-Saw
and run for president
make promises to cure
the country's problems
heal the country's sick

(let's see if they think I'm God)
fix the country's death-of-it
(better take a trip back to Kansas
do some more women and write another book,
I'm gonna need some more dinero to pull this one off)
Yeah, I'm your man
I've got the perfect plan
Vote for me
and I'll fix everything
You'll see
Elected, Alright, Yeeeeehaaaaaw
(stupid suckers)

Or maybe I'll just stay at home
write poetry and promote peace
(Yeah that's what I'll do)

I AM A LAB RAT

The maze is endless
from cradle to death,
government experimental
with every last breath.
Laboratory rodents
facing struggles and strives,
while political scientists,
keeping fucking with our lives.

Feed us some cheese,
and see if we die.
Take away our dignity,
and see if we cry.
Study our habits,
our wants and desires,
then pull out our teeth
with your little metal pliers.
Feed our wives to Boots,
and neuter us all
to see if we decrease
or grow fat and tall.

Yes, pleasure us, torture us,
while you still can,
for one day among us
you will stand,
thrown from your pedestal
with a mighty crash,
and when it happens,
we're gonna tear you a new ass.

THE CIRCUS

Every four years,
As routinely as the moon,
The great elites gather,
To plot our annual doom.
'Tis a festive event,
And like sheep we flock,
To watch as the wolves,
Kiss ass and talk their talk.

Oh, the stunts they are amazing,
Though we've seen them all before,
Once again, we sit in awe,
And wonder what's in store,
As an elephant in a tutu,
Dances a political jig,
Promises tax decreases,
And tells of a deficit big,
And an ass in opposition,
Not to be outclassed,
Gathers in his herd,
And they all get fucking smashed.

Yes, a festive occasion, indeed,
They pull out all the stops,
And come November 5th,
We poor ignorant sops,
Gather for the slaughter,
In booths from shore to shore,
And cast our ballets for the butcher,
Who next we shall endure …

… And thus another circus,
            Draws slowly to an end,
And we the sheep wander off,
Knowing we've just been fucked again.

PRACTICE MAKES PERFECT

abeunt studia in mores

Indoctrinated in perjury
By universities of politics
You laugh at my people
Tell them to:
Refrain from manufacturing
Elongated bridges
Out of little mounds
Thrown up
By burrowing insectivores.

I'd like to slip you a Mickey Finn,
Laced with LSD and a serum of veracity,
Set back and smoke a joint
And watch you,
As you fuck yourselves into oblivion.

WORMS

The morning sun struggling to peek
  over the horizon in the east,
Slowly awakens the worms in the
  belly of the beast,
Wiggling, squirming from
  their comfy little beds,
Jumping, running, to and fro,
  out of their heads.
Must hurry! Must hurry!
  The rats begin to scurry,
And the worms rushing headlong,
  begin to fret and worry.
The rat race is on,
  the trophy the dollar,
The early worm gets the bird,
  What a hoot! What a holler!
Because in the end,
  the worms feed on the carcasses,
That once were us,
And the sun,
  rises in the east,
On a new generation of worms
  in the belly of the beast.

THE FORGOTTEN LEGIONS OF SPARTICUS

A quarter of a century has passed me by,
As self-sympathetic and pitiful, I lie,
Cursing society's conformities and the world as a whole,
While sadistic, paganistic aristocrats took their toll,
On the helpless, vulnerable, unarmed common man.
Carefully they carried out their malicious plan,
Upon the botched and the bungled of the land,
And as we looked up in a bewildered daze,
They attempted to console us with this phrase,
"The world is a stage and we merely players in it."
Bullshit! The world is an apartment and we merely tenants,
Living in your cockroach villas and your slums,
Taking each day by day as it comes,
Dreaming, always dreaming of that day,
When your arrogant heads at our feet will lay,
Severed from your worthless carcasses
By us, the forgotten legions of Sparticus.

A TOUCH OF SPIRITUALITY

From a poetic standpoint, I often feel like I do not write enough poems on this subject. I think it is because I have very little trouble expressing my thoughts and opinions on spirituality when asked, while some of the other topics in this book are easier for me to deal with through the eyes of a poet.

My first poem "Death Too Soon" was written after a friend of mine died in childbirth. She was sixteen. Several months after her death, I was still struggling, grasping for reasons. Now I realize writing that poem was the start of my self-therapy, or maybe a better term would be poetic therapy. The next day, I wrote another poem. It would be nearly two years before I wrote a third poem, but over the years, I have turned to poetry often when I needed an outlet for my emotions.

I was nineteen when I wrote that first poem, now thirty-five years later, I have found a kind of spiritual peace that I did not know then. It took quite a journey through a variety of religions and ultimately the realization that religion is a group effort while spirituality is much more personal before I found peace.

As I have said in previous sections of this book, I do not have all the answers, as a matter of fact, I probably have more questions now than I have ever had, but then I believe that is the way it is meant to be. Physically there comes a time when we cease to grow, but spiritually speaking we should continue to learn and grow throughout our lives. Looking back, which I try not to do too often, there are whole periods of my life where there was absolutely no spiritual growth and while this is probably very common for folks my age, I still find it saddens me.

EQUAL IN HIS EYES

Around the corner and down the hall,
About chest high upon the wall,
A message for all who pass,
An answer to the question they've ask,
"Who is the greatest of us all?",
And the answer there upon the wall,
The One who put us here below,
And caused our breath and blood to flow,
Yes, He's the greatest of us all,
It is written there upon the wall.
It leaves no place for prejudice,
Only room for love, hope, and fairness,
For it is written on the wall,
Around the corner and down the hall.
None here have lesser or greater worth,
All come from the same mud and earth,
And He loves us and watches overall.
His name is there, upon the wall.

WHEN DEATH COMES CALLING

Will we be ready,
  When death comes calling?
Will we go quietly,
  Or be dragged away bawling?

'Tis a scary thought,
  That haunts the minds of all.
What will our lot be,
  When the Maker comes to call?

Did I live right,
  While at my earthly home?
What will become of me,
  When I pass into that great unknown?

These thoughts plague the best of souls,
  And turn them into crazy men.
Perhaps we should live as best we can,
  And not be afraid of the end.

For God alone knows what,
  Lays ahead for you...and for me.
On earth live as his servant,
  And in death He shall set you free.

DEATH TOO SOON
(In memory of Marcie)

A soft mound of earth,
A child fresh from birth.
She the setting sun,
His life just begun.
All too often seen,
A mother at sixteen.
The scorn she couldn't bear,
And so, she fled from here.
A lover, and a son,
Her life over—done.
Some were quick to say,
"God willed it that way!"
Maybe they were wrong,
Does God really shorten life's song?
Could prejudice—pride—
Be the reasons she died?

MEMORIES

We live imperfect lives,
   In an imperfect world.
Always hoping - striving,
   For perfection -
But it never comes.

Ashes to ashes,
   Dust to dust,
To our death beds we go -
   Still hoping -
   Still striving.

A memory is all
   We leave behind
And in time it too
   Fades Away …

GOD OR NOT

Thou shalt not lie, cheat, or have a wild fling.
Who commanded this, God of James the king?
Is the black book laying on our nightstands,
Just a good story or the law of the land?
Was Darwin right? Do we all come from apes?
Or were we placed here by a God that's great?
When to the Grim Reaper or breath we sell,
Will we go to a heaven or a hell?
Or simply be laid in a cold dark grave?
This question turns us humans into slaves,
Searching for an answer we'll never find,
Stumbling through our lives as though we were blind,
Choosing science or faith in the Lord our God.
'Tis a tough choice, which pathway will we trod?
On the one hand there's God, Faith knows him well.
On the other, science, where there's no hell.
In choosing the first, when we do die,
Disappointed we'll be, if in graves we lie,
But if the other hand should be our choice,
There will be no call for us to rejoice,
If at death, judgment awaits. For whom will we tell?
There are no atheists *living* in hell.

LESSONS OF LIFE

Learn not only from your own mistakes,
But from those of others,
True love is a rarity,
Do not be fooled by infatuation,
Put a little back for a rainy day,
Speak softly and listen to what others have to say,
The river of life runs swiftest in the middle,
Stay close to the banks and you'll live longer
and see more of the view.
The leather faced old man, hardened by life's heartaches,
Callused by life's many pitfalls, in a gruff aged voice,
Continued his lessons of life.
The rebellious, deafened by superior wisdom, intellect and
knowledge, youth
With the "youth will conquer all" attitude, tuned him out.

In thirty years, the youth will have become the old man,
Hardened by life, he will teach his lessons of life,
To a rebellious, deafened by superior wisdom, intellect and
knowledge, youth
With a "youth will conquer all" attitude, who will tune him out.

And thirty years further on, that youth will have become,
The old man, hardened by life, teaching his lessons of life
    to a rebellious ...

THE OLD LADY

In a corner she sits
Weaving with ancient hands
The world's loneliest lady
Known through all the lands.
Her needle, the wind,
The falling rain, her tears.
She grows more wrinkled
With the passage of years.
She is forever gentle,
And mighty and bold.
She is so young and new,
And yet, so, very, very old.
Childless she weeps,
For barren is she,
And yet, she is Mother
To everyone you see.

'tis there I'll fly

Can you imagine a place
      where time has no place,
Where a minute doesn't matter,
And seconds don't exist?
Where a walk
      takes an eternity,
And the days never end?
Where Love is like raindrops
      that fall from the sky
And water the Spirits
      as they pass by?
I can …
  I can imagine that place,
I can …
  I can feel the rain on my face,
And some day soon …
      'tis there I'll fly.

POEMS THAT DIDN'T FIT ANYWHERE ELSE

I don't know how it is for other poets but for myself inspiration can come from some pretty unlikely places. Once after watching a show on killers who suffered from schizophrenia, I picked up a pencil and paper and started jotting down lines. Another time, while urinating in a Port-A-Potty at one of those little carnivals that you find in small towns, I was shocked by the way that some of the solid materials floating in the blue water looked like little heads. How could one possibly pass up a chance to put such an emotional experience into verse?

I have ADHD. I may have mentioned that already. It has been my experience in life that because of the way my mind works, if a creative idea crosses my mind, I can either do something about it or ignore it. The problem with ignoring it is that it then becomes a runaway squirrel inside my head. What do I mean by that? Some squirrels people with ADHD see in passing. Those pesky little critters grab your attention momentarily and then they are gone. But runaway squirrels are a different kind of creature. They make laps inside your head. Sometimes really quickly, sometimes rather slowly, but always, until you take care of them, they circle. There have been times, one of these runaway squirrels has nestled down and hidden in the recesses of my mind for many years, only to spring forth with its little furry tail swishing as if to say "Walla!!! I'm back!!!"

So, I feel completely comfortable placing the blame for the poems in this section on those runaway squirrels. Enjoy the squirrels.

DESTINATION UNKNOWN

An army of ants march across the hot concrete,
Detouring around a young child's feet,
Destination unknown.

inside the mind of a schizophrenic

well - my body killed her -
yeah - but i wasn't there -
well - maybe i was there -
yeah - and i lost hair -
elvis lost his too,
but he wasn't there -
but maybe he did it -
yeah - she was a slut
you know - billy the kid -
yeah - he was a nut,
maybe he did it,
but i didn't do it -
you think i did it -
well, you're full of shit -
you see - no, no - see,
i mean - we can see,
i couldn't have done it -
the devil talked to me,

but i didn't listen,
because he's crazy -
no he didn't do it,
he's way to lazy -
yeah - he used my body,
he made me do it,
but i wasn't even there -
not even a little bit -
elvis - and the devil,
i think they did it,
or even billy the kid -
yeah, maybe that's it -
they all had a plan,
and they all killed her -
or maybe i did,
my body was there -

JOHN CLAY

A fine white snow gently covered the ground,
And soft north winds knocked pinecones down.
From the top of a spruce covered rise,
The old cowboy sat his horse. He's eyes
Scanned the beautiful spread below.
The cattle, as they moved to and fro,
Searching for grass beneath the snow,
Stirring memories of long ago.

An old man's face slowly approached,
His gruff old voice softly coached,
"Cattle are fine, as long as their fed,
But men should enjoy 'fore their dead.
Don't live life to fast, nor to slow,
And you'll be happy when you go."
The old man had been right, somehow,
Yes, he could see that clearly now.
Life wasn't something you could outrun,
Nor something you could wait on to come,
You simply maintained a good pace,
And life would stay right in your face.

Being in the dusk of his life,
The old cowboy had a home, a good fine wife,
And three sons to carry on his name,
Done over, he'd do it all the same.
Night was coming upon him fast,
But he had to do one last task.
Turning his horse, he started down,
Smiling at the snow-covered ground.
Life had been good to him, no doubt.
He knew his time was nearly out,
And he wished to tell his wife, Sue,
That his love for her was still true.

He was almost to the front yard,
When the pain struck him, sharp and hard,
His chest began to throb and heave,
His breath began to slowly leave,
And then he saw his wife's strong face,
Like an angel sent with Heaven's grace,
Shining through the darkness. He spoke,
"I love you...always will." Then choked,
With the last breath he'd ever take,
Darkness came like a cold damp lake,
And as he died, he hear her say,
"I love you... always will, John Clay."

JOHNNY AND THE GENERAL

A drunken young sailor did quickly appear,
When the stripper called for someone to kiss her rear.
She cocked her hip out and flipped up her skirt,
As the fellow's companions yelled, "Don't get hurt!"
"Come on Johnny kiss that butt!"
And Johnny smiled and puckered up.
He had just placed his lips on her soft lovely rear,
When somebody shouted, "Attenshut!! The general is here!"
The young sailor, filled with anxiety and fear,
Quickly removed his lips from her beautiful rear,
Stepped back sharply, and said,
   "Here's where the line begins."
The aged general looked startled,
   as he scratched his chin.
   "Your next, Sir, so dive right in.
   It's okay, just kiss her rear-end."
The general examined the young lasses butt,
Then to the surprise of his men, he puckered up.
The moral of the story is here at last,
Even an old general sometimes must kiss some ass.

INTOXICATED MEDITATION

a ½ gallon of hard liquor
(Jim Beam perhaps)
a pack of smokes
(or a joint or two)
drink the liquor quickly
until the room begins to spin
like a Vegas roulette wheel
7 – 4 – 3 – Black 13
now have a smoke
let the room come to
a stand still
have a seat or set up
clear your mind
you are now thoughtless
meditating on utter emptiness
completely void
or perhaps passed out cold
setting there stoned off your ass
and intoxicated.

ME, MYSELF, AND Y

Alone at last.
Just the three of us.
Someone put out the
DO NOT DISTURB sign,
And we'll have a
conversational threesome,
an orgy of thoughts.

One, you are the
rebel, the stud,
the "I'll do or
try anything once."
being in this
unlikely group.

Two, you are the
prude, the "goody-
two-shoes", the
weigher of right,
the conscience
in a group that
neither wants
or likes you.

Three, you are
the peace-maker,
the go between,
the cement that
binds all together,
without you this
little group would
disintegrate into
utter despair.

Together we are one,
Together we are awesome,
The Three Musketeers,
Indestructible.

Three as one,
One is two,
Two is three,
And three is one,
But why?

PORT-A-POTTIE DREAMS

Six thousand tiny heads
floating in a hole,
filled with shit, piss,
and cheap toilet paper,
singing life's songs,
I saw the crack of Dawn
and it went on and on ...
(a laugh, a snicker, some hisses)
It's raining, it's pouring
and some lucky smuck is scoring
To each his/her own
A golden flow
just made their day
(sick puppies/insane sex/kinky,
You should try it)
Hey who turned out the lights,
Oh shit, IT'S AN ASS, BIG TURD,
Dodge, Run, Move, Too Late,
Life's a shit sandwich
and the bread is cheap toilet paper
for six thousand tiny heads
floating in a Port-A-Pottie.

PSYCHIC CALLS

I've got runners in my hose,
And earrings in my nose,
And my balls itch all the time.
The phone rings off the walls,
With continuous creditor calls,
And I can't find a fucking dime.
My doctors say I'm dying,
And the baby won't stop crying,
But my psychic says everything's fine.
If I knew what the future would bring,
I'd do the right thing,
And shot the bitch for $3.99,
But I'd probably get rich and well,
And my life'd be shot to hell,
'Cause I'd be in jail
for something that shouldn't be a crime.

WRITING & WHY I DO IT

Change! Is that not why all poets write? Perhaps not, but for the most part this is why I put pencil to paper, scribbling my thoughts out on the page. So, what is it I want changed. Ultimately, everything that is not right in the world, but then who gets to decide what is right? And what is wrong? What matters? And what does not matter?

You do. I do. We do. And sometimes, yes, even they do. Often in this every changing world it is so easy to get caught up in the machinery that is society that we simply forget that we are not just another cog in it but human beings with hopes, dreams, and desires. In the big picture, I write because I wish to make changes and a small part of me still believes that there is a chance that one of the poems I have written will inspire a change that brings about world peace and universal happiness. Okay, maybe that is a bit ambitious, but I can hope.

Did I mention that I have ADHD? And a slight case of OCD? Well, I do. Another reason, I write is because for me it is therapeutic. It helps me deal with myself. Not an easy task, if you do not believe me just ask those who have had to deal with me for over half a century.

If I had to give one reason, and only one, for why I write, it would be because I love to do it. And why I write poems is simple. Poetry has always come much easier to me than novels. Over the years I have written hundreds of poems. In that same time, I have managed to finish only a few novels. Whether it be poems, or short stories, or full-length books, I will continue to write as long as the love for it remains. And should it ever vanish, well, I guess, I will cease to write.

THE POEM

You criticize my poem,
  Because it has no meter.
Go screw yourself,
  You dead horse beater!
I write my poem
  As it comes,
And thrill in it
  When it's done.
You write you poem
  As you will,
For me your poem
  Has no thrill.
I leave your poetry to you,
  Leave mine to me.
Each to write his own
  For all eternity.

WHY I WRITE

The memories of a few great souls,
  Remain long after their bodies have rotted,
But for the most of mankind,
  They simply live out the lives they're allotted,
And as their bodies rot away,
  Their memories do the same.
These simple forgettable souls,
  Are the people from whence I came.
In confession, I know little
  Of my family tree,
And so, by writing, I hope for
  Eternal Immortality.

THE GREAT POETIC PLAGUE

Jazz killed itself
But don't let poetry kill itself
                    Jack Kerouac

Jack, jazz is dead
I can't bring it back
But I won't let poetry die

I breath, it breaths
    like a *Taenia* in my gut
I breath, it grows
    and through me
    it will infect others
It will spread like a plague
The great poetic plague

It will spread, infecting all
    all those Wharton pioneers
    all those Pound pushers
    all those ANTI-BEAT maniacs
That refuse to read your poems
            refuse to join your movement
I will infect them all
And poetry will live and grow
And the BEAT will go on
            sure as shit.

TO AND FOR ALLEN GINSBERG & JACK KEROUAC

As I sit here
reading your poetry
in books I found in a store
hidden behind a Wal-Mart
I begin to think
of college literature classes.
I light up another cheap
generic cigarette and inhale.
I'm pissed.
I read your poems
inhaling each word
each line like my
burning cigarette
and experience a poetic high
that I can find in no other
poet's work.
Why then I ask myself and
whoever is crazy enough to
listen to me
do they not expose us
to this magnificent intoxicating poetry
in our literature classes.

Poetry is life
and life is poetry
I tell my professors
and they laugh
and pound Pound into my head.

WHY????!!!WHY???!!!WHY???!!!
One professor did stop Pounding
long enough to ask
if those beat poets were so great
why do we not hear more about them today
it was just a movement let it fade
but you haven't faded
you are alive running through my head
and each night I sit and smoke
and read and get my poetic fix
your movement lives on
and as long as there are beat junkies
like myself there will always be a place
for your poetry to roam and it will not
fade, IT WILL NOT FADE!!!

THE PICASSO IN ME

Pen and ink
Sits gathering dust.
My mind, stagnating,
Begins to rust.
Two years
Pass slowly by,
And then ...
An innocent look,
A chance touch,
And charm
Like a gentle breeze,
Awakes the dormant embers,
Deep inside.
Slowly stoking
With intelligence and care
Until a small flame appears
And grows and grows ...
And awakens
   the Picasso in me.

RHYTHMS

From the grave
    to the cradle
        to the egg,
The best part
    ran down your momma's leg,
And if you believe a word I've said,
You ought to have some quack
        examine your head,
Because the drums that beat
          in your mind,
Are gyrating a rhythm I just can't find,
Which doesn't make you or me,
        less or more,
It just means we each chose
        a different door,
And we each must deal
      with what's behind,
So, you deal with your fucked up life,
      and let me deal with mine.

NOT YOUR AVERAGE CHRISTMAS POEMS

"Jake's Night Before Christmas" is my favorite Christmas poem. My Dad, Charles C. Brown, wrote it when I was very young, and when I was in high school, I memorized it and recited it at speech tournaments. I never won any awards for it, mainly because it was funny and the poems that won were often sad and dramatic.

I have not written many Christmas poems myself and none as epic as Dad's, but I thought I might as well share them with you. Enjoy.

CHRISTMAS

Christmas is over
  and Ol' Saint Nick has finally flown home,
Leaving us here
  with sagging tree, otherwise alone,
And as we pull the plug
  on yet another holiday filled with cheer,
One must wonder,
  if indeed we've learned anything this year,
And, if in the year ahead,
  we will more Christ-like become,
Or simply, continue in
  our merry little search for wealth and power and fun.
Christmas,
  the birthday of our Savior and Lord,
Or just, one more holiday,
  we can no longer afford.
Mr. Atheist and Mr. Baptist and Mr. Catholic and Mr. All,
  I offer you a thought to ponder
as the Christmas snow thaws.
  Is this a holiday essential to our salvation,
Or simply a brilliant ideal from the figments
  Of a shrewd businessman's imagination?

Two Nights before Christmas

'Twas two nights before Christmas at ole Saint Nick's house,
And he was mad as hell, and needing to get soused
But the liquor cabinet was empty and his stash was all gone,
So, he sat by the Christmas tree, sad and alone.
The missus was off to another craft show,
And when she'd be back, he really didn't know.
The elves where all tinkering away in the shop,
And all he really wanted was just one little shot,
Some Gentleman Jack poured over ice,
Two fingers of Johnnie Walker Red sure sounded nice.
Wild Turkey or Jameson or even some Crown,
But no matter where he looked there was none to be found.
The rein deer all bedded down snug in their stalls,
Had no idea he was having withdrawals,
When he stumbled through the door and out into the cold
With nary a plan, if the truth be told.
To the reindeer shed he trudged through the snow,
His jacket pulled snug and his head hanging low.
He slammed through the door with such a clatter,
That the reindeer all rose to see what was the matter.
With a wave of his hand, he sent them back to bed,
Then looked all around and scratched his ole head.
Surely, somewhere there's a bottle I've stashed,
And round and round the shed he dashed.
He looked in his sack, He looked in his sleigh,
In a sack of reindeer feed and behind some hay,

And for an instance he thought it was but a dream,
For there behind the straw, a full bottle of Jim Beam.
Oh, his eyes how they twinkled, his cheeks all a flush,
And he opened that bottle in quite a rush.
One shot, two shot, three shot, four,
And after that, he poured him one more,
And before he knew it that the bottle was dry,
And shouted to the reindeer,
Ho! Ho! Ho! Bitches, it's time to fly.
Out of the shed and up over the roofs,
They disappeared in flurry a of hooves,
Leaving him standing there in bourbon bliss,
And so, this Christmas 'it is what it is".
So, Fly away Etsy, and Amazon Prime,
Up, Up, and away it's Walmart.com time.
On Ebay! On Sears! On Target and Kohls?
A quick stop at the Dollar Tree for paper and bows,
And, gift cards galore stuffed into cards,
Cause shopping this year is just too freakin' hard.
The rein deer are missing, gone into the night,
And Santa is still in no shape for flight.
So, to one and all, it's purely academic,
Ole Saint Nick just ain't doing well with this here pandemic,
But he had something he thought you needed to hear,
Merry Christmas to all, and to all a Happy New Year?

IN THE BEGINNING:

In the mid-nineties, I put toget-
her a small pamphlet of some of
my poems and handed them
out. Things were very different
then. After much trial-and-error,
I managed to get the pages all in
the correct places and printed
them on my home computer. I
then had to hand staple each
little booklet myself. And while
this is my first official volume
of poetry, I will always think of
that little booklet as my first
attempt at truly being a poet.

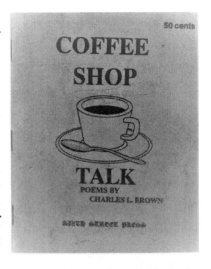

It was called "Coffee Shop Talk" and even though the price
of fifty cents was printed on the front covers, most of them were
given away. I did, however, have one young lady insist that I take
two quarters for the one I gave her, and I did as she asked. I would
like to say I still have those quarters safely hidden away some-
where, but alas, I do not. My mother is fond of telling people that
if you get paid for doing something that makes you a professional.
If that is true, then I guess my writing career actually started in
1996 and I have truly been a starving poet/artist for over a quarter
of a century.

A second volume called "Coffee Shop Talk II" was planned
but got derailed before it ever got completed. Life can be tricky
that way. In honor of my humble beginnings, I decided to include
the poems from that publication in this volume.

COFFEE SHOP TALK

Gossip flows free as water,
No one is spared the slaughter,
Be ye, waitress, or teacher,
Doctor, lawyer, or preacher.
Prejudice, slander abounds,
And yet, neither has any bounds,
For color, age, sex, nor race,
Will keep your name from this place.
As black as the brew served here,
Whispered rumors all will hear,
So, pray you name won't ever drop,
In your local coffee shop.

MISTRESS MAY

Men folks stare as she walks in,
Thoughts turning to pleasures' sin,
Angry wives, cluck and clatter,
Grabbing hubbies, quickly scatter,
Yeah, May Green's a wrecking ball,
Winter, spring, summer, and fall,
Busting marriages, left and right,
With her talents of the night.
Her bed's seldom ever made,
A natural at the trade,
But pleasure, not pay, the reason,
She stays open all season.

WELFARE WILMA

More cash she'll see, if not praise,
'Cause very soon she'll get a raise,
For you see, Wilma Sliver,
At any moment will deliver,
One more baby to be fed,
Or so somebody said,
By the people of this state,
See what some laws create?
What is this one, nine, or ten?
And then she'll do it again,
For it's the business she's in,
That in itself is her only sin.

THE DUCHESS

A diamond on each finger,
Proves she's a real humdinger,
She strolls through town aloft,
With an air that tees most off,
Be it money or her raisin',
That makes the biddy so brazen,
Us common folks will never know,
For we are much too far below,
The level at which a return,
Bring her worry or concern,
Mere droppings upon the street,
To be smashed beneath her feet.

THE DOCTOR

No need to overreact,
If you happen to contract,
The common cold or the flu,
Doctor Don will doctor you.
Bottoms which he's had to slap,
He's seen more than ol' Santas' lap,
But the ones he most adores,
Are the ladies that come
    through his doors,
For whatever their ailment be,
It's their nakedness he must see,
Before he will ever be sure,
That he's found the correct cure.

THE PREACHER

Sweet sermons, gives Preacher Paul,
The sweetest, but that's not all,
'Cause little Miss Mary Vixen,
In a few short months is fixin',
Whether by immaculate means,
Or realistic extremes,
To deliver a brand-new life,
And she's neither girlfriend nor wife,
But only a close friend it seems,
Since she's only just turned sixteen,
To our very good Preacher Paul,
Who is now the talk of all.

THE LAWYER

If it's time for you to sue,
Or if someone's suing you,
You'll need representation.
He's got the reputation,
Of being fast, just, and fair,
However, don't take your wife there.
For Larry is very good in courts,
But he's a ladies' man of sorts.
Given a case he'll do just great,
But there are those who would state,
With his love of skirts and fun,
More harm than good, he has done.

THE WAITRESS

"She's a tramp," the ladies say,
"And will be 'til her dying day."
But the men simply adore,
The way she crosses the floor,
Bringing menu, drink, or food,
Always friendly, never rude,
And she bends and stoops a lot,
Giving all a cleavage shot,
Which irritates hubbies' mates,
Who throw her looks of hate,
But she ignores the angry wives,
'Cause hubbies tip, not with ones,
                          but fives.

WIDOW GLASS

The Old Widow Peggy Glass,
Friday before last,
Did a little air let pass,
Not a scandal, but alas,
By Monday, it was the talk,
In every coffee shop.
Old Mr. Moore,
      who heard it first,
Was just about to burst,
When Joey came walking in,
So, he told Joey,
      And Joey told Ben …
And when noontime hit,
That little fart,
Had become a full-blown shit.

COFFEE SHOP TALK II

Have a seat and prop your feet up,
Grab a cigarette and a coffee cup,
Yeah, it's time for another round,
Oh, the gossip in this town,
And if you listen you will hear,
The scoop from far away and very near.
Maybe it ain't front page news,
Or even worthy of reviews,
But to those who frequently stop,
At their local coffee shop,
The whispered rumors you will hear
Are as vital as the brew served here.

LETTER TO THE READERS

Thank You. With your assistance, whether you read one of the poems in this book or each and every one of them, you, as the reader, have helped to complete the journey. My part in the trip was to capture the squirrels and turn them into words on the page, and I did the best I could to tame as many of the little critters as possible. But like a zoo with no visitors, this book would be a very sad place for poems to dwell if you had not come along to read them. So, once again, *Thank You.*

In addition to you, the reader, I would like to thank my parents, Carolyn Brown and Charles C. Brown. They are the driving force behind my writing career. By example they have taught me what hard work and diligence can accomplish. Without Mom's, you can do it peptalks, I fear the critters would have fled the zoo long before this book was completed. And of course, Dad's love of poetry and songwriting took root deep within me long ago and has only grown through the years. I would have to say that it was the seed that started this whole project, so a special Thanks to Dad for passing on those genetics.

The dedication page of this work of poetry says, "To Whom It May Concern" and there is good reason behind it. Many of the poems throughout this book were inspired by someone specific. Others came to be because of something someone said. More than a few of the poems within this volume I still have deep connections to because of the emotions behind them and the memories they generate each time I read them. So, without naming names, whether you made me feel loved, or broke my heart, or simply by word, deed, or action, inspired one of these poems, Thank You.

Last, but definitely not least, I want to thank the wonderful lady who formats my books. Without her help I would be totally lost. Thank You, Judi Fennell, for the outstanding job you do and for your patience and willingness to work around my ADHD and OCD. You are truly appreciated.

Until next time,

Charles Lemar Brown

ABOUT THE AUTHOR

Charles Lemar Brown is a retired high school science teacher, who now spends much of his time writing and traveling. In addition to this work, he has also published three novels, The Road to Nowhere, The Neon Church Journal, and The Seventh Date, as well as, a book of short stories entitled Raised Redneck, Vol. 1. He is also an avid photographer whose photographs have  been sold around the world. He lives in rural Love County, Oklahoma, where he enjoys spending time with his seven children and nineteen grandchildren. Left alone too long, he is likely to be found writing, working out in his home gym, or kicked back with his cat, Tilee, watching whatever football game he can find on the television. His favorite quote is—what doesn't kill you makes you stronger and I ain't dead yet.

Made in the USA
Columbia, SC
27 September 2023

23435306R00107